Casual Weekend
KNITS

LEISURE ARTS, INC. • Maumelle, Arkansas

What better way is there to spend the weekend than to cozy up with a new knitting project? As a relaxing and creative outlet, knitting has the ability to provide the well needed break from the hustle and bustle of daily life. It still amazes me how with only two needles and some yarn, we have the ability to create an endless variety of beautiful garments and accessories, each with its own unique style and charm.

My design process always begins with the yarn. Upon seeing and feeling its texture and characteristics, it inspires my decision as to the type of project it will become and the specific stitches I will use. I find my designs are also influenced by my experiences, travels and architecture. Personally, I mostly enjoy the types of projects that can be finished in no more than a few days.

Casual Weekend Knits is an exciting collection of scarves, cowls, shawls, hats and more, knit with a selection of wonderful yarns. Each project provides the opportunity to utilize stylish, yet not overly difficult knitting patterns and techniques. You will be able to create exciting new designs with remarkable textures you'll love to knit and wear (or give to a special someone).

I wish to share with you my love for the craft, and hope you are inspired by these designs to take out your needles and start a new knitting adventure.

Knit, wear, and enjoy!

Andi Javori

Asymmetrical Shawl

 **EASY**

Finished Size: 15" deep (at widest point) x 68" long (38 cm x 173 cm)

SHOPPING LIST

Yarn (Medium Weight)

[5 ounces, 250 yards
(141 grams, 228 meters) per skein]:
☐ MC (Grey) - 2 skeins
[6 ounces, 315 yards
(170.1 grams, 288 meters)
per skein]:
☐ CC (Bright Green) - 1 skein

Knitting Needle

24" (61 cm) Circular,
☐ Size 9 (5.5 mm)
   or size needed for gauge

GAUGE INFORMATION

In Garter Stitch (knit every row),
   16 sts and 24 rows = 4" (10 cm)

TECHNIQUES USED

- YO *(Fig. 3a, page 76)*
- kfb *(Figs. 4a & b, page 76)*
- pfb *(Fig. 5, page 76)*
- K2 tog *(Fig. 9, page 77)*

When instructed to slip a stitch, always slip as if to **purl** *(Fig. A).*

Fig. A

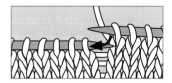

SHAWL

With MC, cast on 3 sts.

Row 1: K1, kfb, k1: 4 sts.

Row 2 (Right side)**:** Kfb, K1, K2 tog.

Row 3: Slip 1, K1, kfb, K1: 5 sts.

Row 4: Kfb, K2, K2 tog.

Row 5: Slip 1, K2, kfb, K1: 6 sts.

Row 6: Kfb, knit across to last 2 sts, K2 tog.

Row 7 (Increase row)**:** Slip 1, knit across to last 2 sts, kfb, K1: 7 sts.

Rows 8-25: Repeat Rows 6 and 7, 9 times: 16 sts.

Cut old color when changing to a new color.

Row 26: With CC, kfb, knit across to last 2 sts, K2 tog.

Row 27: Slip 1, purl across to last 2 sts, pfb, P1: 17 sts.

Row 28: Kfb, (YO, K2 tog) across to last 2 sts, K2 tog.

Row 29: Slip 1, purl across to last 2 sts, pfb, P1: 18 sts.

Row 30: With MC, kfb, knit across to last 2 sts, K2 tog.

Row 31 (Increase row)**:** Slip 1, knit across to last 2 sts, kfb, K1: 19 sts.

Rows 32-45: Repeat Rows 30 and 31, 7 times: 26 sts.

Rows 46-225: Repeat Rows 26-45, 9 times: 116 sts.

Bind off all sts in **knit**.

Bias Scarf

◼◻◻◻◻ **BASIC**

Finished Size: 7" wide x 72" long (18 cm x 183 cm)

SHOPPING LIST

Yarn (Medium Weight) 🧶**4**
[5 ounces, 251 yards
(142 grams, 230 meters) per skein]:
☐ Color A (Black) - 1 skein
☐ Color B (Red) - 1 skein
☐ Color C (Grey) - 1 skein
☐ Color D (Light Grey) - 1 skein

Knitting Needles
☐ Size 10 (6 mm)
   or size needed for gauge

GAUGE INFORMATION
In Garter Stitch (knit every row),
   18 sts and 32 rows = 4" (10 cm)

TECHNIQUES USED
• kfb (*Figs. 4a & b, page 76*)
• K2 tog (*Fig. 9, page 77*)

Scarf consists of eight 9" (23 cm) blocks measured across the side edge. It can easily be made shorter by making the blocks smaller than 9" (23 cm), just be sure to knit all of the blocks the same size.

SCARF

With Color A, cast on 38 sts.

First Block

Row 1 (Right side)**:** With Color A, kfb, knit across to last 2 sts, K2 tog.

Row 2: Knit across.

Repeat Rows 1 and 2 for pattern until First Block measures approximately 9" (23 cm) along side edge, ending by working Row 2.

Cut Color A.

Second Block

With Color B, repeat Rows 1 and 2 of First Block until Second Block measures approximately 9" (23 cm) along side edge, ending by working Row 2.

Cut Color B.

Third Block

With Color C, repeat Rows 1 and 2 of First Block until Third Block measures approximately 9" (23 cm) along side edge, ending by working Row 2.

Cut Color C.

Fourth Block

With Color D, repeat Rows 1 and 2 of First Block until Fourth Block measures approximately 9" (23 cm) along side edge, ending by working Row 2.

Cut Color D.

Work First through Fourth Blocks once **more**; at end of the Fourth Block, do **not** cut Color D.

Bind off all sts in **knit**.

Bobble Cowl

Finished Size: 7" tall x 27" circumference (18 cm x 68.5 cm)

SHOPPING LIST

Yarn (Bulky Weight) 🧶 **5**
[8.8 ounces, 466 yards
(250 grams, 426 meters) per skein]:
☐ 1 skein

Knitting Needles
☐ Size 11 (8 mm)
or size needed for gauge

Additional Supplies
☐ Yarn needle

GAUGE INFORMATION
In Stockinette Stitch
(knit one row, purl one row),
12 sts and 16 rows = 4" (10 cm)
In pattern, 28 sts = 6½" (16.5 cm)

TECHNIQUE USED
• P3 tog (*Fig. 14, page 78*)

COWL
Cast on 30 sts.

Row 1 (Right side)**:** Purl across.

Row 2: K1, ★ (K1, P1, K1) **all** in the
next st, P3 tog; repeat from ★ across
to last st, K1.

Row 3: Purl across.

Row 4: K1, ★ P3 tog, (K1, P1, K1) **all** in
the next st; repeat from ★ across to
last st, K1.

Repeat Rows 1-4 for pattern until
piece measures approximately 27"
(68.5 cm) from cast on edge **or** to
desired length, ending by working a
wrong side row.

Bind off all sts in **purl**, leaving a long
end for sewing

Fold piece in half with **wrong** side
together. Using long end and
matching cast on edge with bind off
edge, sew seam.

Boot Cuffs

 EASY

SHOPPING LIST

Yarn (Medium Weight) 🧶4
[4 ounces, 203 yards
(113 grams, 186 meters) per skein]:
☐ 1{1-2-2} skein(s)

Knitting Needle
16" (40.5 cm) Circular,
☐ Size 8 (5 mm)
or size needed for gauge

Additional Supplies
☐ Stitch marker
☐ Cable needle

SIZE INFORMATION
Finished Measurements:
12{14½-17-19½}" circumference x
6½{6½-7-7}" tall
30.5{37-43-49.5} cm x
16.5{16.5-18-18} cm

Size Note: We have printed the
instructions for the sizes in different
colors to make it easier for you to
find:
• size Small in Blue
• size Medium in Pink
• size Large in Green
• size X-Large in Purple
Instructions in Black apply to all sizes.

Cuffs tend to stretch when worn.

GAUGE INFORMATION
In Stockinette Stitch
  (knit every round),
  20 sts and 24 rnds = 4" (10 cm)

STITCH GUIDE
CABLE 4 FRONT *(abbreviated C4F)*
  (uses next 4 sts)
Slip next 2 sts onto cable needle and
hold in **front** of work, K2 from left
needle, then K2 from cable needle.
CABLE 4 BACK *(abbreviated C4B)*
  (uses next 4 sts)
Slip next 2 sts onto cable needle and
hold in **back** of work, K2 from left
needle, then K2 from cable needle.

BOOT CUFF (Make 2)

Cast on 60{72-84-96} sts *(Fig. 1, page 75)*; place a marker to indicate the beginning of the round *(see Markers, page 75)*.

Rnds 1-6: (K2, P2) around.

Rnd 7: Knit around.

Rnd 8: ★ (K1, P1) 2{4-6-8} times, K4, C4B, C4F, K4; repeat from ★ 2 times **more**.

Rnd 9: ★ (P1, K1) 2{4-6-8} times, K 16; repeat from ★ 2 times **more**.

Rnd 10: ★ (K1, P1) 2{4-6-8} times, K2, C4B, K4, C4F, K2; repeat from ★ 2 times **more**.

Rnd 11: ★ (P1, K1) 2{4-6-8} times, K 16; repeat from ★ 2 times **more**.

Rnd 12: ★ (K1, P1) 2{4-6-8} times, C4B, K8, C4F; repeat from ★ 2 times **more**.

Rnd 13: ★ (P1, K1) 2{4-6-8} times, K 16; repeat from ★ 2 times **more**.

Rnds 14 thru 37{37-43-43}: Repeat Rnds 8-13, 4{4-5-5} times.

Next Rnd: Knit around.

Next 6 Rnds: (K2, P2) around.

Bind off all sts in pattern.

Choker & Bracelet

■■□□ EASY

SHOPPING LIST

Yarn (Fine Weight) [2] FINE
[1.75 ounces, 202 yards
(50 grams, 185 meters) per skein]:
☐ 1 skein will make **both**

Knitting Needles
☐ Size 6 (4 mm)
or size needed for gauge

Additional Supplies
☐ 11 mm Decorative buttons -
3 for **each** design
☐ Sewing needle and
matching thread

GAUGE INFORMATION
Gauge is not necessary for these
projects but they should be knit
tightly.

*Both designs tend to stretch a little
when worn. They both easily can be
made to any lengths.*

Finished Measurements:
Choker - 2" wide x 15" long (5 cm x 38 cm)
Bracelet - 2" wide x 6½" long (5 cm x 16.5 cm)

TECHNIQUES USED
• YO *(Figs. 3a & b, page 76)*
• K2 tog *(Fig. 9, page 77)*

CHOKER/BRACELET
Cast on 13 sts.

Rows 1 and 2: Knit across.

Row 3: (Buttonhole row): (K2, YO,
K2 tog) 3 times, K1.

Rows 4 and 5: Knit across.

Row 6: Purl across.

Row 7 (Right side)**:** P2, ★ YO, slip 1 as
if to **purl** *(Fig. A)*, K2, PSSO 2 sts just
made; repeat from ★ 2 times **more**,
P2.

Repeat Rows 6 and 7 until piece
measures approximately 6" (15 cm)
for the Bracelet and 14½" (37 cm)
for the Chocker **or** to desired length
minus ½" (12 mm), ending by
working a **right** side row.

Last 4 Rows: Knit across.

Bind off all sts in **knit**.

Sew decorative buttons onto the end
opposite buttonholes.

Fig. A

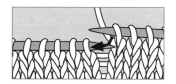

Chunky Scarf

◼◻◻◻ **BASIC**

Finished Size: 8" wide x 64" long (20.5 cm x 162.5 cm)

SHOPPING LIST

Yarn (Super Bulky Weight) **6** SUPER BULKY
[6 ounces, 106 yards
(170 grams, 97 meters) per skein]:
☐ 2 skeins

Knitting Needles
☐ Size 17 (12.75 mm)
or size needed for gauge

GAUGE INFORMATION
In Stockinette Stitch
(knit one row, purl one row),
8 sts and 12 rows = 4" (10 cm)
In pattern, 18 sts = 8" (20.5 cm)

SCARF
Cast on 18 sts.

Row 1 (Right side)**:** Knit across.

Row 2: (K3, P3) across.

Rows 3-8: Repeat Rows 1 and 2, 3 times.

Row 9: Knit across.

Row 10: (P3, K3) across.

Rows 11-16: Repeat Rows 9 and 10, 3 times.

Repeat Rows 1-16 for pattern until Scarf measures approximately 64" (162.5 cm) from cast on edge **or** to desired length.

Bind off all sts in pattern.

Headband

◼◻◻◻ **BASIC**

Finished Size: 5" wide x 18" circumference unstretched (12.5 cm x 45.5 cm)

SHOPPING LIST

Yarn (Medium Weight) **4** MEDIUM
[3.5 ounces, 207 yards
(100 grams, 190 meters) per skein]:
☐ 1 skein

Knitting Needles
☐ Size 8 (5 mm)
  or size needed for gauge

Additional Supplies
☐ Yarn needle

GAUGE INFORMATION

In Stockinette Stitch
  (knit one row, purl one row),
  20 sts and 24 rows = 4" (10 cm)

TECHNIQUES USED

- YO (*Fig. 3a, page 76*)
- kfb (*Figs. 4a & b, page 76*)
- K2 tog (*Fig. 9, page 77*)

HEADBAND

Cast on 16 sts.

Rows 1 and 2: Knit across.

Row 3 (Right side)**:** K1, (YO, K2 tog) across to last st, k1.

Rows 4-6: Knit across.

Row 7: Kfb across: 32 sts.

Row 8: Purl across.

Row 9: Knit across.

Row 10: Purl across.

Rows 11-13: Knit across.

Rows 14-16: Repeat Rows 8-10.

Row 17: K2 tog across: 16 sts.

Row 18: Purl across.

Work Rows 1-18, a **total** of 7 times
[8 times if you need to add an
additional 2½" (6.5 cm) to the
circumference].

Bind off all sts in **knit** leaving a long
end for sewing.

Thread yarn needle with long end.
With **right** side together, sew cast on
edge and bound off edge together.

Lace Fingerless *Gloves*

 **EASY**

Finished Size: 7" circumference x 8½" long (18 cm x 21.5 cm)

SHOPPING LIST
Yarn (Medium Weight) **4 MEDIUM**
[4 ounces, 203 yards
(113 grams, 186 meters) per skein]:
☐ 1 skein

Knitting Needles
☐ Size 7 (4.5 mm) **and**
☐ Size 8 (5 mm)
   or sizes needed for gauge

Additional Supplies
☐ Yarn needle

GAUGE INFORMATION
In Stockinette Stitch
   (knit one row, purl one row),
   18 sts and 24 rows = 4" (10 cm)

TECHNIQUES USED
• YO *(Fig. 3a, page 76)*
• K2 tog *(Fig. 9, page 77)*
• slip 1, K1, PSSO *(Figs. 11a & b, page 77)*

GLOVE
Cuff
With smaller size needles and leaving a long end for sewing, cast on 35 sts.

Row 1 (Right side)**:** K1, (P1, K1) across.

Row 2: P1, (K1, P1) across.

Rows 3-6: Repeat Rows 1 and 2 twice.

Body
Change to larger size needles.

Row 1 (Right side)**:** K4, YO, K2, slip 1, K1, PSSO, K2 tog, K2, ★ YO, K1, YO, K2, slip 1, K1, PSSO, K2 tog, K2; repeat from ★ once **more**, YO, K5.

Row 2: Purl across.

Repeat Rows 1 and 2 until piece measures approximately 7½" (19 cm)

from cast on edge, ending by working a **purl** row.

Ribbing
Change to smaller size needles.

Row 1 (Right side)**:** K1, (P1, K1) across.

Row 2: P1, (K1, P1) across.

Rows 3-6: Repeat Rows 1 and 2 twice.

Bind off all sts in pattern. Cut yarn, leaving a long end for sewing.

Thread yarn needle with long end and sew seam from bind off edge for 1¼" (3 cm).

Thread yarn needle with cast on end and sew seam from bottom of Cuff for 5¾" (14.5 cm), leaving a thumb opening.

Lace Hat

 **EASY**

Finished Size: 8½" high x 18" circumference (21.5 cm x 45.5 cm)

GAUGE INFORMATION
With larger size needles,
  in Stockinette Stitch
  (knit one row, purl one row),
  18 sts and 24 rows = 4" (10 cm)

TECHNIQUES USED
- YO (*Fig. 3a, page 76*)
- K2 tog (*Fig. 9, page 77*)
- slip 1, K1, PSSO (*Figs. 11a & b, page 77*)

HAT
Ribbing
With smaller size circular needle, cast on 90 sts (*Fig. 1, page 75*); place a marker to indicate the beginning of the round (*see Markers, page 75*).

Rnd 1 (Right side)**:** (K1, P1) around.

Repeat Rnd 1 until Ribbing measures approximately 1" (2.5 cm) from cast on edge.

Body
Change to larger size circular needle.

Rnd 1 (Right side)**:** Knit around.

Rnd 2: ★ YO, K2, slip 1, K1, PSSO, K2 tog, K2, YO, K1; repeat from ★ around.

Repeat Rnds 1 and 2 until piece measures approximately 6½" (16.5 cm) from cast on edge.

SHAPING

*Change to double-pointed needles when there are too few stitches to use a circular needle (**see Double-Pointed Needles, page 75**).*

Rnd 1: Knit around.

Rnd 2: (K7, K2 tog) around: 80 sts.

Rnd 3: Knit around.

Rnd 4: (K6, K2 tog) around: 70 sts.

Rnd 5: Knit around.

Rnd 6: (K5, K2 tog) around: 60 sts.

Rnd 7: Knit around.

Rnd 8: (K4, K2 tog) around: 50 sts.

Rnd 9: (K3, K2 tog) around: 40 sts.

Rnd 10: Knit around.

Rnd 11: (K2, K2 tog) around: 30 sts.

Rnds 12: (K1, K2 tog) around: 20 sts.

Rnd 13: Knit around.

Rnd 14: K2 tog around: 10 sts.

Cut yarn leaving a long end for sewing.

Thread yarn needle with long end and slip remaining sts onto yarn needle; pull **tightly** to close and secure end.

Lacy Cowl

◼◼◻◻ **EASY**

Finished Size: 7" tall x 28" circumference (18 cm x 71 cm)

SHOPPING LIST

Yarn (Medium Weight) 🧶**4**
[3.5 ounces, 207 yards
(100 grams, 190 meters) per skein]:
☐ 1 skein

Knitting Needle

29" (73.5 cm) Circular,
☐ Size 10 (6 mm)
  or size needed for gauge

Additional Supplies

☐ Stitch marker

GAUGE INFORMATION

In Stockinette Stitch (knit every rnd),
  16 sts and 20 rnds = 4" (10 cm)

TECHNIQUE USED

• YO *(Fig. 3a, page 76)*

COWL

Cast on 108 sts *(Fig. 1, page 75)*; place a marker to indicate the beginning of the round *(see Markers, page 75)*.

Rnds 1-4: (K2, P2) around.

Rnd 5: Knit around.

Rnd 6: (YO, K4) around: 135 sts.

Rnd 7: ★ YO, drop the next st off the left needle, slip 1 as if to **knit**, K3, PSSO 3 sts just made; repeat from ★ around: 108 sts.

Rnds 8 and 9: Knit around.

Rnds 10-33: Repeat Rnds 6-9, 6 times.

Rnds 34-37: (K2, P2) around.

Bind off all sts in **knit**.

Long Two-Color *Cowl*

BASIC

Finished Size: 7½" tall x 52" circumference (19 cm x 132 cm)

GAUGE INFORMATION

In pattern (Rnds 16-25),
  12 sts = 4" (10 cm);
  9 rnds = 1¼" (3.25 cm)

TECHNIQUES USED

• YO *(Fig. 3a, page 76)*
• K2 tog *(Fig. 9, page 77)*

COWL

With MC, cast on 160 sts *(Fig. 1, page 75)*; twisting sts **once** around the needle, place a marker to indicate the beginning of the round *(see Markers, page 75)*.

Rnd 1 (Right side)**:** Knit around.

Rnd 2: Purl around.

Rnd 3: (YO, K2 tog) around.

Rnds 4-15: Repeat Rnds 1-3, 4 times.

Cut old color when changing to a new color.

Rnds 16-19: With CC, knit around.

Rnds 20-25: With MC, repeat Rnds 1-3 twice.

Rnds 26-29: With CC, knit around.

Rnds 30-32: With MC, repeat Rnds 1-3.

Rnds 33-46: Repeat Rnds 16-25 once, then repeat Rnds 16-19 once **more**.

Rnds 47-59: With MC, repeat Rnds 1-3, 4 times; then repeat Rnd 1 once **more**.

Bind off all sts in **purl**.

Poncho *Top*

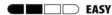 **EASY**

SHOPPING LIST

Yarn (Medium Weight) [4]
[3.5 ounces, 218 yards
(100 grams, 199 meters) per skein]:
- ☐ Color A (Teal) -
  {3-3-3}{3-4-4-4} skeins
- ☐ Color B (Light Grey) -
  {3-3-3}{3-4-4-4} skeins

Knitting Needles
- ☐ Size 10 (6 mm)
  or size needed for gauge

Additional Supplies
- ☐ Stitch markers - 2
- ☐ Yarn needle

SIZE INFORMATION

Measurements:
Actual Bust:
{32-34-38}{40-43-46-49}"/
{81.5-86.5-96.5}
{101.5-109-117-124.5} cm

Finished Length:
{22-23-24}{25-26-27-28}"/
{56-58.5-61}{63.5-66-68.5-71} cm

Size Note: We have printed the instructions for the sizes in different colors to make it easier for you to find:
- size Small in Blue
- size Medium in Pink
- size Large in Green
- size X-Large in Purple
- size 1X in Red
- size 2X in Dark Green
- size 3X in Dk Blue

Instructions in Black apply to all sizes.

GAUGE INFORMATION

In Stockinette Stitch
  (knit one row, purl one row),
  18 sts and 24 rows = 4" (10 cm)

STITCH GUIDE

KNOT (uses 3 sts)
Purl 3 sts together leaving the sts on the left needle, yarn around the right needle, then purl the same 3 sts together again slipping the sts off the left needle.

TECHNIQUE USED

- YO *(Fig. 3c, page 76)*
- pfb *(Fig. 5, page 76)*
- K2 tog *(Fig. 9, page 77)*
- P3 tog *(Fig. 14, page 78)*

PANEL (Make 2)
Bottom Border

With Color A, cast on {121-127-145}{151-163-175-187} sts.

Rows 1-16: K1, (P1, K1) across.

Lower Body

Row 1 (Right side): K1, (P1, K1) 5 times, PM, knit across to last 11 sts, PM, K1, (P1, K1) 5 times.

Row 2: K1, (P1, K1) across to next marker, SM, purl across to next marker, SM, K1, (P1, K1) across.

Row 3: K1, (P1, K1) across to next marker, SM, knit across to next marker, SM, K1, (P1, K1) across.

Repeat Rows 2 and 3 until piece measures approximately {11-11½-12}{12½-13-13½-14}"/{28-29-30.5}{32-33-34.5-35.5} cm from cast on edge ending by working a **wrong** side row; cut Color A.

Upper Body

Row 1 (Right side): With Color B, K1, (P1, K1) across to next marker, SM, knit across to next marker decreasing one st, SM, K1, (P1, K1) across: {120-126-144}{150-162-174-186} sts.

Row 2: K1, (P1, K1) 5 times, SM, P1, work Knots across to within one st of next marker, P1, SM, K1, (P1, K1) across.

Row 3: K1, (P1, K1) across to next marker, SM, knit across to next marker, SM, K1, (P1, K1) across.

Row 4: K1, (P1, K1) across to next marker, SM, purl across to next marker, SM, K1, (P1, K1) across.

Row 5: K1, (P1, K1) across to next marker, SM, knit across to next marker, SM, K1, (P1, K1) across.

Repeat Rows 2-5 for pattern until Upper Body measures approximately {8¾-9¼-9¾}{10¼-10¾-11¼-11¾}"/{22-23.5-25}{26-27.5-28.5-30} cm, ending by working a **right** side row.

Increase Row: K1, (P1, K1) across to next marker, SM, purl across to next marker increasing one st, SM, K1, (P1, K1) across: {121-127-145}{151-163-175-187} sts.

Top Border

Rows 1-16: K1, (P1, K1) across.

Bind off all sts in pattern.

With **wrong** sides of Panels together and using Color B, sew shoulders leaving a {10-10-10}{11-11-12-12}"/{25.5-25.5-25.5}{28-28-30.5-30.5} cm neck opening.

Poncho

 **BASIC**

SHOPPING LIST

Yarn (Medium Weight) 4
[4 ounces, 203 yards
(113 grams, 186 meters) per skein]:
- ☐ MC (Blue) - 3 skeins
- ☐ CC (Grey) - 1 skein

Knitting Needles
- ☐ Size 11 (8 mm)
  or size needed for gauge

Additional Supplies
- ☐ Yarn needle

SIZE INFORMATION

Finished Measurements:
48{54}" x 22{26}"/
122{137} cm x 56{66} cm

Size Note: We have printed the instructions for the sizes in different colors to make it easier for you to find:
- size Small/Medium in Pink
- size Large/X-Large in Purple
Instructions in Black apply to both sizes.

GAUGE INFORMATION

In Garter Stitch (knit every row),
14 sts and 24 rows = 4" (10 cm)

*Do **not** cut yarn unless otherwise specified.*

FIRST STRIPED SECTION

With MC, cast on 70{82} sts.

Rows 1 and 2: Knit across.

Row 3 (Right side)**:** With CC, knit across.

Row 4: Purl across.

Rows 5 and 6: With MC, knit across.

Repeat Rows 3-6 for pattern until Striped Section measures approximately 12{14}"/30.5{35.5} cm from cast on edge, ending by working Row 4; cut CC.

GARTER SECTION

With MC, work in Garter Stitch until Garter Section measures approximately 24{28}"/61{71} cm, ending by working a **wrong** side row.

LAST STRIPED SECTION

Row 1 (Right side)**:** With CC, knit across.

Row 2: Purl across.

Rows 3 and 4: With MC, knit across.

Repeat Rows 1-4 for pattern until Last Striped Section measures approximately 12{14}"/30.5{35.5} cm, ending by working Row 4 (should have the same number of rows as the First Striped Section); cut CC.

Bind off all sts in **knit**, leaving a long end for sewing.

Fold piece in half with **wrong** side and Striped Sections together. Thread yarn needle with long end and sew end of rows of Striped Sections together, leaving Garter Section unsewn for neck opening.

Purse

 **EASY**

Finished Size: 13" wide x 10" deep (33 cm x 25.5 cm)

SHOPPING LIST

Yarn (Medium Weight) [4]
[3 ounces, 145 yards
(85 grams, 133 meters) per skein]:
☐ 3 skeins

Knitting Needles
☐ Size 8 (5 mm)
   or size needed for gauge

Additional Supplies
☐ Cable needle
☐ Fabric for lining (a few inches
   larger than the bag)
☐ Interfacing material -
   Pellon Peltex 70 Ultra Firm
   Stabilizer - (optional to line
   and make bag firm)
☐ Clasp
☐ Sewing needle and
   matching thread
☐ Yarn needle

GAUGE INFORMATION

In Stockinette Stitch
   (knit one row, purl one row),
   17 sts and 24 rows = 4" (10 cm)

TECHNIQUE USED

• K2 tog *(Fig. 9, page 77)*

STITCH GUIDE

CABLE 4 FRONT *(abbreviated C4F)*
   (uses next 4 sts)
Slip next 2 sts onto cable needle and
hold in **front** of work, K2 from left
needle, then K2 from cable needle.

CABLE 4 BACK *(abbreviated C4B)*
   (uses next 4 sts)
Slip next 2 sts onto cable needle and
hold in **back** of work, K2 from left
needle, then K2 from cable needle.

PURSE

Panel (Make 2)
Beginning at bottom edge,
cast on 68 sts.

Row 1: Purl across.

Row 2 (Right side)**:** K1, P3, K4, (P4, K4)
across to last 4 sts, P3, K1.

Row 3: Purl across.

Rows 4-7: Repeat Rows 2 and 3
twice.

Row 8: K4, (P4, K4) across.

Row 9: Purl across.

Row 10: K2, (C4F, C4B) across to last
2 sts, K2.

Row 11: Purl across.

Rows 12-61: Repeat Rows 2-11, 5 times.

TOP BORDER

Row 1 (Right side): Knit across.

Row 2: P1, knit across to last st, P1.

Row 3: K2 tog, (K4, K2 tog) across: 56 sts.

Row 4: P1, knit across to last st, P1.

Row 5: Knit across.

Row 6: P1, knit across to last st, P1.

Row 7: (K2 tog, K6) across: 49 sts.

Bind off all sts in **knit**.

Handle (Make 2)
Cast on 5 sts.

Work in Garter Stitch (knit every row) until Handle measures approximately 20" (51 cm) **or** to desired length, taking into consideration that the Handle tends to stretch when Purse is carried.

Bind off all sts in **knit**.

Finishing
With **right** sides facing, sew bottoms of the Panels together.

With **wrong** side facing, place interfacing material about ½" (12 mm) from the sides and 1" (2.5 cm) from the top, stitch in place. (Since the material lining will cover it, you can just sew it at the corners.) Place material lining over interfacing material about ¼" (6 mm) from the sides and about 1" (2.5 cm) from the top and sew it in place on all sides of the Purse.

With **wrong** sides together, sew side seams.

It's optional to sew lining on one side of the Handles before sewing them in, since they tend to stretch when Purse is carried.
Sew Handles to Purse approximately 2½" (6.5 cm) from **each** edge.
Attach clasp to center of inside of Purse.

Short Scarf

◼◼◻◻ **EASY**

Finished Size: 7" wide x 33" long (18 cm x 84 cm)

SHOPPING LIST
Yarn (Medium Weight) **4**
[5 ounces, 251 yards
(142 grams, 230 meters) per skein]:
☐ 1 skein
Knitting Needles
☐ Size 9 (5.5 mm)
 or size needed for gauge
Additional Supplies
☐ Yarn needle

GAUGE INFORMATION
In Stockinette Stitch
 (knit one row, purl one row),
 18 sts and 24 rows = 4" (10 cm)

TECHNIQUES USED
- YO (*Fig. 3a, page 76*)
- kfb (*Figs. 4a & b, page 76*)
- K2 tog (*Fig. 9, page 77*)
- P2 tog (*Fig. 10, page 77*)
- slip 1, K2 tog, PSSO (*Figs. 13a & b, page 78*)

SCARF
Band
Leaving a long end for sewing, cast on 20 sts.

Row 1: Purl across.

Row 2 (Right side): K1, ★ YO, K2, pass YO on right-hand needle over 2 sts just made; repeat from ★ across to last st, K1.

Repeat Rows 1 and 2 until Band measures approximately 6" (15 cm) from cast on edge, ending by working a **purl** row.

Increase Row: Knit across increasing 9 sts evenly spaced (*see Increasing Evenly Across a Row/Round, page 77*): 29 sts.

Next Row: Purl across.

Body
Row 1 (Right side): K4, YO, slip 1, K2 tog, PSSO, ★ YO, K3, YO, slip 1, K2 tog, PSSO; repeat from ★ 2 times **more**, YO, K4.

Row 2: Purl across.

Row 3: K1, YO, slip 1, K2 tog, PSSO, ★ YO, K3, YO, slip 1, K2 tog, PSSO; repeat from ★ 3 times **more**, YO, K1.

Row 4: Purl across.

Repeat Rows 1-4 for pattern until piece measures approximately 35¼" (89.5 cm) from cast on edge, ending by working a **purl** row.

Next Row: K1, K2 tog across: 15 sts.

Next Row: P1, P2 tog across: 8 sts.

Next Row: K2 tog across: 4 sts.

Last Row: Knit these 4 sts together *(Fig. A)*; cut yarn and draw end through remaining st.

Fig. A

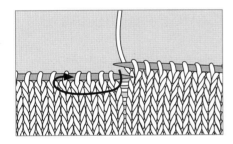

With **wrong** side together, fold Band in half and, with long end, sew cast on edge to base of increase row to form a loop.

 **EASY**

SHOPPING LIST

Yarn (Medium Weight) 🔵**4**
[5.3 ounces, 312 yards
(150 grams, 285 meters) per skein]:
☐ {2-2}{2-3-3} skeins

Knitting Needle
32" (81.5 cm) Circular,
☐ Size 10½ (6.5 mm)
or size needed for gauge

Additional Supplies
☐ 5 - Decorative buttons
(optional)
☐ Sewing needle and matching
thread (if using optional
buttons)

SIZE INFORMATION
Finished Measurements:
{17-18}{19-20-21}" long x
{40-44}{48-52-56}" circumference/
{43-45.5}{48.5-51-53.5} cm x
{101.5-112}{122-132-142} cm

Size Note: We have printed the
instructions for the sizes in different
colors to make it easier for you to find:
- size X-Small in Red
- size Small in Blue
- size Medium in Pink
- size Large in Green
- size X-Large in Purple
Instructions in Black apply to all sizes.

GAUGE INFORMATION
In Stockinette Stitch
(knit one row, purl one row),
16 sts and 20 rows = 4" (10 cm)

TECHNIQUE USED
- K2 tog *(Fig. 9, page 77)*

SHRUG
Beginning at bottom edge,
cast on {136-148}{160-172-184} sts.

Rows 1-5: Knit across.

Row 6 (Wrong side)**:** Purl across.

Rows 7-9: Knit across.

Repeat Rows 6-9 for pattern until piece measures approximately {14-15}{16-17-18}"/{35.5-38} {40.5-43-45.5} cm from cast on edge, ending by working a **purl** row.

Maintain established pattern throughout.

Decrease Row: K4, (K2 tog, K4) across: {114-124}{134-144-154} sts.

Continue in pattern for 1½" (4 cm).

Decrease Row: K4, (K2 tog, K3) across: {92-100}{108-116-124} sts.

Continue in pattern for 1½" (4 cm).

Decrease Row: K3, K2 tog, (K2, K2 tog) across to last 3 sts, K3: {70-76} {82-88-94} sts.

Continue in pattern for 1-1½" (2.5-4 cm), ending by working a **purl** row.

Top Border
Rows 1–6: Knit across.

Bind off all sts in **knit**.

Side Band
With **right** side facing, pick up sts evenly across end of rows *(Fig. 15, page 78)*.

Rows 1-5: Knit across.

Bind off all sts in **knit**.

Repeat across opposite side of Shrug.

Sew side seam from Top Border to about half way down the Shrug.

Using photo as a guide for placement, add buttons if desired.

Slip-Stitch Scarf

◖☐☐☐▱ **BASIC**

Finished Size: 6¼" wide x 60½" long (16 cm x 153.5 cm)

SHOPPING LIST
Yarn (Medium Weight) ⓸
[4 ounces, 203 yards
(113 grams, 186 meters) per skein]:
☐ MC (Blue) - 1 skein
[3.5 ounces, 166 yards
(100 grams, 151 meters) per skein]:
☐ CC (Variegated) - 1 skein

Knitting Needles
☐ Size 10½ (6.5 mm)
or size needed for gauge

GAUGE INFORMATION
In Stockinette Stitch
(knit one row, purl one row),
16 sts and 20 rows = 4" (10 cm)

*When instructed to slip a stitch, always
slip as if to **purl** (Fig. A).*

SCARF
With MC, cast on 27 sts.

Row 1: (Right side): Knit across.

Row 2: Purl across.

Row 3: With CC, K1, (slip 1 wyib, K3)
across to last 2 sts, slip 1 wyib, K1.

Row 4: K1, (slip 1 wyif, K3) across to
last 2 sts, slip 1 wyif, K1.

Rows 5 and 6: Repeat Rows 3 and 4.

Fig. A

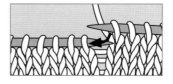

Row 7: With MC, knit across.

Row 8: Purl across.

Row 9: With CC, K3, (slip 1 wyib, K3)
across.

Row 10: K3, (slip 1 wyif, K3) across.

Rows 11 and 12: Repeat Rows 9 and
10.

Row 13: With MC, knit across.

Repeat Rows 2-13 for pattern until
piece measures approximately 60"
(152.5 cm) from cast on edge **or** to
desired length; cut CC.

Last Row: Purl across.

Bind off all sts in **knit**.

Small Clutch

 **EASY**

Finished Size: 10" wide x 6" deep (25.5 cm x 15 cm)

SHOPPING LIST

Yarn (Medium Weight) **MEDIUM 4**
[4 ounces, 203 yards
(113 grams, 186 meters) per skein]:
☐ 1 skein

Knitting Needles

☐ Size 8 (5 mm)
    or size needed for gauge

Additional Supplies

☐ Yarn needle
☐ Fabric for lining
☐ 9" (23 cm) Zipper
☐ Sewing needle and
    matching thread

GAUGE INFORMATION

In pattern (Rows 1 and 2),
    30 sts = 4" (10 cm)

TECHNIQUES USED

• YO *(Fig. 3a, page 76)*
• P2 tog *(Fig. 10, page 77)*

PANEL (Make 2)

Beginning at bottom edge, cast on 72 sts.

Row 1 (Right side): K1, ★ slip 1 as if to **knit**, K1, YO, pass slipped st over the st **and** the YO on right needle; repeat from ★ across to last st, K1.

Row 2: ★ P2 tog **without** dropping both sts from left needle, then purl the **first** st again slipping both sts off the left needle; repeat from ★ across.

Repeat Rows 1 and 2 until piece measures approximately 6" (15 cm) from cast on edge, ending by working Row 1.

Bind off all sts as follows:

P1, ★ P2 tog, you now have 2 sts on the right needle, with the left needle, pass the back st on the right needle over the front st and completely off the right needle, removing the left needle from the st; repeat from ★ across to last st, purl and bind off last st.

FINISHING

With **right** sides facing, sew bottoms of the Panels together.

With **wrong** side facing, place lining about ¼" (6 mm) from the side edges and sew the lining in place (not the top).

With **wrong** sides together, sew side seams.

Place zipper at top of bag and sew in place. Sew the lining across the top, partially covering the edges of the zipper.

Textured Scarf

EASY

Finished Size: 5¾" wide x 62" long (14.5 cm x 157.5 cm)

SHOPPING LIST

Yarn (Medium Weight) **4 MEDIUM**
[5 ounces, 251 yards
(142 grams, 230 meters) per skein]:
☐ 2 skeins

Knitting Needles
☐ Size 9 (5.5 mm)
or size needed for gauge

GAUGE INFORMATION

In Stockinette Stitch
(knit one row, purl one row),
18 sts and 24 rows = 4" (10 cm)

TECHNIQUES USED

• YO *(Fig. 3a, page 76)*
• K2 tog *(Fig. 9, page 77)*
• slip 1, K1, PSSO *(Figs. 11a & b, page 77)*

SCARF

Cast on 29 sts.

Rows 1-4: Knit across.

Row 5 (Right side): K8, P1, (K5, P1) twice, K8.

Row 6: K3, P5, (K1, P5) 3 times, K3.

Row 7: K3, YO, slip 1, K1, PSSO, P1, K2 tog, ★ YO, K1, YO, slip 1, K1, PSSO, P1, K2 tog; repeat from ★ 2 times **more**, YO, K3.

Row 8: K3, P2, K1, (P5, K1) 3 times, P2, K3.

Row 9: K5, (P1, K5) across.

Row 10: K3, P2, K1, (P5, K1) 3 times, P2, K3.

Row 11: K3, K2 tog, YO, K1, YO, slip 1, K1, PSSO, ★ P1, K2 tog, YO, K1, YO, slip 1, K1, PSSO; repeat from ★ 2 times **more**, K3.

Row 12: K3, P5, (K1, P5) 3 times, K3.

Repeat Rows 5-12 for pattern until piece measures approximately 61¼" (155.5 cm) from cast on edge, ending by working a **wrong** side row.

Last 4 Rows: Knit across.

Bind off all sts in **knit**.

Trellis Scarf

◼◻◻◻◻ **BASIC**

Finished Size: 7" wide x 60" long (excluding fringe) (18 cm x 152.5 cm)

SHOPPING LIST
Yarn
(Super Bulky Weight) **6** SUPER BULKY
[6 ounces, 106 yards
(170 grams, 97 meters) per skein]:
☐ Color A (Off White) - 1 skein
(Medium Weight) **4** MEDIUM
[1.75 ounces, 140 yards
(50 grams, 128 meters) per skein]:
☐ Color B (Variegated) - 1 skein
Knitting Needles
☐ Size 15 (10 mm)
or size needed for gauge
Additional Supplies
☐ Crochet hook (for fringe)

GAUGE INFORMATION
In pattern (Rows 3-6),
   15 sts = 7" (18 cm);
   16 rows = 4" (10 cm)

SCARF
With Color A, cast on 15 sts.

Rows 1 and 2: Knit across.

Drop unused color and carry yarn up edge of Scarf.

Rows 3 and 4: With Color B, knit across.

Rows 5 and 6: With Color A, knit across.

Repeat Rows 3-6 for pattern until Scarf measures approximately 60" (152.5 cm) from cast on edge, **or** to desired length, ending by working Row 6.

Bind off all sts in **knit**.

Fringe

Holding Color A and Color B together, cut 56 (28 pairs), **each** 14" (35.5 cm) long.

Hold together 2 strands of **each** color; fold in half.

With **wrong** side of Scarf facing, insert crochet hook into one of the corners. Draw the folded ends through far enough to pull the loose ends through the folded end **(Fig. A)**. Draw the knot up **tightly (Fig. B)**. Repeat, placing fringe approximately ½" (12 mm) apart, until 7 groups have been placed at both ends of Scarf.

Fig. A

Fig. B

Triangle *Shawl*

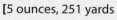 **EASY**

Finished Size: 31" long x 68" wide (78.5 cm x 172.5 cm)

SHOPPING LIST

Yarn (Medium Weight) **4**
[5 ounces, 251 yards
(142 grams, 230 meters) per skein]:
☐ Color A (Red) - 2 skeins
☐ Color B (Tan) - 2 skeins

Knitting Needle

32" (81.5 cm) Circular,
☐ Size 10 (6 mm)
or size needed for gauge

Additional Supplies

☐ Stitch markers - 2

GAUGE INFORMATION

In Stockinette Stitch
(knit one row, purl one row),
16 sts and 20 rows = 4" (10 cm)

TECHNIQUES USED

- kfb *(Figs. 4a & b, page 76)*
- M1L *(Figs. 6a & b, page 76)*
- M1R *(Figs. 7a & b, page 76)*

SHAWL

With Color A, cast on 3 sts.

Row 1: (Right side)**:** Kfb, PM, K1, PM, kfb: 5 sts.

Row 2: Purl across.

Row 3: Kfb, K1, M1R, SM, K1, SM, M1L, K1, kfb: 9 sts.

Row 4: Purl across.

Row 5: Kfb, K3, M1R, SM, K1, SM, M1L, K3, kfb: 13 sts.

Row 6: Purl across; cut Color A.

Row 7: With Color B, kfb, knit across to next marker, M1R, SM, K1, SM, M1L, knit across to last st, kfb: 17 sts.

Row 8: Knit across; cut Color B.

Row 9: With Color A, kfb, knit across to next marker, M1R, SM, K1, SM, M1L, knit across to last st, kfb: 21 sts.

Row 10: Purl across.

Rows 11-14: Repeat Rows 9 and 10 twice; at end of Row 14, cut Color A: 29 sts.

Row 15: With Color B, kfb, knit across to next marker, M1R, SM, K1, SM, M1L, knit across to last st, kfb: 33 sts.

Row 16: Knit across.

Rows 17 and 18: Repeat Rows 15 and 16; at end of Row 18, cut Color B: 37 sts.

Rows 19-26: Repeat Rows 9 and 10, 4 times; at end of Row 26, cut Color A: 53 sts.

Rows 27-32: Repeat Rows 15 and 16, 3 times; at end of Row 32, cut Color B: 65 sts.

Rows 33-42: Repeat Rows 9 and 10, 5 times; at end of Row 42, cut Color A: 85 sts.

Rows 43-50: Repeat Rows 15 and 16, 4 times; at end of Row 50, cut Color B: 101 sts.

Rows 51-62: Repeat Rows 9 and 10, 6 times; at end of Row 62, cut Color A: 125 sts.

Rows 63-72: Repeat Rows 15 and 16, 5 times; at end of Row 72, cut Color B: 145 sts.

Rows 73-86: Repeat Rows 9 and 10, 7 times; at end of Row 86, cut Color A: 173 sts.

Rows 87-98: Repeat Rows 15 and 16, 6 times; at end of Row 98, cut Color B: 197 sts.

Rows 99-114: Repeat Rows 9 and 10, 8 times; at end of Row 114, cut Color A: 229 sts.

Rows 115-128: Repeat Rows 15 and 16, 7 times; at end of Row 128, cut Color B: 257 sts.

Rows 129-146: Repeat Rows 9 and 10, 9 times; at end of Row 146, do **not** cut Color A: 293 sts.

Rows 147 and 148: With Color A, repeat Rows 15 and 16: 297 sts.

Bind off all sts in **purl**.

Shaded Cowl

■□□□ **BASIC**

Finished Size: 12" tall x 29" circumference (30.5 cm x 73.5 cm) at bottom and 25" circumference (63.5 cm) at top

SHOPPING LIST

Yarn (Medium Weight) 🧶 **4**
[3.5 ounces, 170 yards
(100 grams, 156 meters)] per skein]:
☐ Color A (Dark Grey) - 1 skein
☐ Color B (Grey) - 1 skein
☐ Color C (Light Grey) - 1 skein

Knitting Needle
24" (61 cm) Circular,
☐ Size 13 (9 mm)
or size needed for gauge

Additional Supplies
☐ Stitch marker

GAUGE INFORMATION

In Seed Stitch pattern (knit the purls and purl the knits as they face you), 12 sts and 22 rnds = 4" (10 cm)

TECHNIQUES USED

- K2 tog (*Fig. 9, page 77*)
- P2 tog (*Fig. 10, page 77*)

COWL

With Color A, cast on 87 sts (*Fig. 1, page 75*); place a marker to indicate the beginning of the round (*see Markers, page 75*).

Rnd 1 (Right side)**:** K1, (P1, K1) around.

Rnd 2: P1, (K1, P1) around.

Repeat Rnds 1 and 2 for Seed Stitch pattern until piece measures approximately 4" (10 cm) from cast on edge, ending by working Rnd 2; cut Color A.

Next Rnd: With Color B, ★ (K1, P1) 12 times, K2 tog, P2 tog; repeat from ★ 2 times **more**, K1, P1, K1: 81 sts.

Beginning with Rnd 2, repeat Rnds 1 and 2 until piece measures approximately 8" (20.5 cm) from cast on edge, ending by working Rnd 2; cut Color B.

Next Rnd: With Color C, ★ (K1, P1) 11 times, K2 tog, P2 tog; repeat from ★ 2 times **more**, K1, P1, K1: 75 sts.

Beginning with Rnd 2, repeat Rnds 1 and 2 until piece measures approximately 12" (30.5 cm) from cast on edge.

Bind off all sts in pattern.

Cabled Mittens

 **EASY**

SHOPPING LIST

Yarn (Medium Weight) **4**
[4 ounces, 203 yards
(113 grams, 186 meters) per skein]:
☐ 1 skein

Knitting Needles
Double-pointed (set of 4),
☐ Size 7 (4.5 mm) **and**
☐ Size 8 (5 mm)
or sizes needed for gauge

Additional Supplies
☐ Cable needle
☐ Split-ring marker
☐ Stitch markers - 2
☐ Stitch holder
☐ Yarn needle

SIZE INFORMATION

Finished Measurements:
7{9}" hand circumference x 10" long/
18{23} cm x 25.5 cm

Size Note: We have printed the
instructions for the sizes in different
colors to make it easier for you to
find:
• size Small/Medium in Pink
• size Large in Green
Instructions in Black apply to both
sizes.

GAUGE INFORMATION

In Stockinette Stitch (knit every rnd),
  20 sts = 4" (10 cm)

TECHNIQUES USED

• kfb (*Figs. 4a & b, page 76*)
• Add on new sts (*Figs. 8a & b,
  page 77*)
• K2 tog (*Fig. 9, page 77*)
• SSK (*Figs. 12a-c, page 78*)

STITCH GUIDE

CABLE 4 FRONT (*abbreviated C4F*)
  (uses next 4 sts)
Slip next 2 sts onto cable needle and
hold in **front** of work, K2 from left
needle, then K2 from cable needle.

CABLE 4 BACK (*abbreviated C4B*)
  (uses next 4 sts)
Slip next 2 sts onto cable needle and
hold in **back** of work, K2 from left
needle, then K2 from cable needle.

MITTEN
Cuff

With smaller size double-pointed needles, cast on 36{48} sts (see **Double-Pointed Needles, page 75**); place a marker to indicate the beginning of the round (see **Markers, page 75**).

Rnds 1-18: (K2, P2) around.

Body

Change to larger size double-pointed needles.

Rnds 1-3: Knit around.

Rnd 4: (K2, C4B) around.

Rnds 5-7: Knit around.

Rnd 8: (C4F, K2) around.

GUSSET

Rnd 1: Knit 18{24} sts, PM, kfb, K1, kfb, PM, knit around: 38{50} sts (5 sts between markers).

Rnd 2: Knit around.

Rnd 3: Knit across to next marker, SM, kfb, knit across to within one st of next marker, kfb, SM, knit around: 40{52} sts (7 sts between markers).

Rnd 4: (K2, C4B) across to next marker, SM, knit across to next marker, SM, K3, (K2, C4B) around.

Rnd 5: Knit across to next marker, SM, kfb, knit across to within one st of next marker, kfb, SM, knit around; 42{54} sts (9 sts between markers).

Rnd 6: Knit around.

Rnd 7: Knit across to next marker, SM, kfb, knit across to within one st of next marker, kfb, SM, knit around: 44{56} sts (11 sts between markers).

Rnd 8: (C4F, K2) across to next marker, remove marker, slip next 11 sts onto st holder, remove marker, **turn work**; add on 3 sts, **turn work**; K3, (C4F, K2) around: 36{48} sts.

HAND

Rnds 1-3: Knit around.

Rnd 4: (K2, C4B) around.

Rnds 5-7: Knit around.

Rnd 8: (C4F, K2) around.

Repeat Rnds 1-8 for pattern until piece measures approximately 1¼" (3 cm) less than desired length.

SHAPING

Rearrange sts on double-pointed needles as needed.

Rnd 1: K 10{14}, PM, K 18{22}, PM, K8{12}.

Rnd 2 (Decrease rnd): ★ Knit across to within 3 sts of next marker, K2 tog, K1, SM, K1, SSK; repeat from ★ once **more**, knit around: 32{44} sts.

Rnd 3: Knit around.

Rnds 4-8: Repeat Rnds 2 and 3 twice, then repeat Rnd 2 once **more**: 20{32} sts.

Rnd 9: Knit around removing markers.

Rnd 10: (K1, K2tog) around to last 2 sts, K2: 14{22} sts.

Rnd 11: K2 tog around: 7{11} sts.

Cut yarn leaving a long end for sewing.

Thread yarn needle with long end and slip remaining sts onto yarn needle; pull **tightly** to close and secure end.

Thumb

Place sts from st holder onto 2 double-pointed needles as follows: Place 5 sts onto Needle 1 and 6 sts onto Needle 2. With Needle 3, pick up 4 sts in the gap where the thumb meets the hand (**Fig. 15, page 78**); place a split-ring marker around the first stitch to indicate the beginning of the round: 15 sts.

Redistribute sts to have 5 sts on each needle.

Rnds 1-5: Knit around.

Rnd 6: K 10, SSK, K1, K2 tog: 13 sts.

Knit around until Thumb measures approximately ¼" (6 mm) less than desired length.

Last Rnd: K1, K2 tog around: 7 sts.

Cut yarn leaving a long end for sewing.

Thread yarn needle with long end and slip remaining sts onto yarn needle; pull **tightly** to close and secure end.